GROWTH OF A TREE

To Dee Ann, May God Bless!

Gene Jenkins

GROWTH OF A TREE

The Journey of a Single Woman

LENA TOMLINSON

TATE PUBLISHING
AND ENTERPRISES, LLC

Growth of a Tree
Copyright © 2014 by Lena Tomlinson. All rights reserved.

No part of this publication may be reproduced, stored in a retrieval system or transmitted in any way by any means, electronic, mechanical, photocopy, recording or otherwise without the prior permission of the author except as provided by USA copyright law.

This book is designed to provide accurate and authoritative information with regard to the subject matter covered. This information is given with the understanding that neither the author nor Tate Publishing, LLC is engaged in rendering legal, professional advice. Since the details of your situation are fact dependent, you should additionally seek the services of a competent professional.

The opinions expressed by the author are not necessarily those of Tate Publishing, LLC.

Published by Tate Publishing & Enterprises, LLC
127 E. Trade Center Terrace | Mustang, Oklahoma 73064 USA
1.888.361.9473 | www.tatepublishing.com

Tate Publishing is committed to excellence in the publishing industry. The company reflects the philosophy established by the founders, based on Psalm 68:11,
"The Lord gave the word and great was the company of those who published it."

Book design copyright © 2014 by Tate Publishing, LLC. All rights reserved.
Cover design by Anne Gatillo
Interior design by Jomar Ouano

Published in the United States of America

ISBN: 978-1-63122-440-9
1. Family & Relationships / Love & Romance
2. Biography & Autobiography / Personal Memoirs
13.04.25

THE JOURNEY OF A SINGLE WOMAN

This is an inspirational book for all single women and men. This book is about my life as a single woman and the trials and tribulations I have undergone leading me to a peaceful content life. I have been a single woman and parent for the last twenty two years. Life has not always been easy for me. God has led me on a roller coaster of highs and lows to self-awareness and self-acceptance.

Living a life of solitude was never in my plans. I want to find unconditional love. I will not lose faith that some day the love of my life will walk through the door. Until that day, I will be content with the person that I have become and the peace that God had instilled in me. He has given me the courage and strength to live a happy and fulfilled life and the independence to do anything my heart desires without fear.

Join me in my journey as a single woman. I hope that it inspires you to be the person that God meant for you to become.

All pictures in this book were taken by the author.

ACKNOWLEDGMENTS

I would like to thank my family and friends for giving me the support and encouragement to write this book. Thank you for always being there for me and encouraging me to be a godly woman. I would like to thank my dear friend Lea Ann Findley not only for her encouragement and support but also for helping me to edit this book. I could not have done this without you. I would also like to thank my friend Marcella Cartwright for her assistance with proofreading.

CONTENTS

Finding Myself 11
Finding My Passion 29
Finding Humanity 65
Finding Memories 81
Finding God's Strength 95

FINDING MYSELF

Strong and *independent* are terms that my friends and family will tell you describe my personality. However, I don't always feel strong and independent on the inside; these are personality characteristics that I have developed over time or rather I have been forced to develop through life experiences. You know what I am talking about; those experiences that have coined the phrase, "If it doesn't kill you, it will just make you stronger."

I have been a single parent for the last twenty-two years. There were only two choices I could have made: take control over my life or roll over and let it take control of me. I choose to take control over my life and live it to the fullest.

I am not someone famous, and I haven't accomplished some amazing feat. I am just your everyday person who has learned to live life to the fullest, *fullest* being a very subjective term; in other words living my life to the fullest may be something completely different than you living your life to the fullest. That being said, I would like to tell you about my journey in life so that maybe you can gain inspiration and take control over your own destiny and embrace life.

I am not going to tell you that life for me has been easy or even fun, but I can tell you that when it is my time to go home to the Lord, I can honestly say that my time on earth was full of rich experiences that made me who I am today.

My hope is that through my adventure, you too can find your own adventure in this wonderful world that God has created for us.

> For I can do everything with the help of Christ who gives me the strength I need. (Philippians 4:13 NLT)

As a warning, I need to tell you that this story is not full of great and spectacular times. I am not going to tell you that if you just follow this recipe for life, you will have everlasting happiness. In fact, I will warn you that some of this story is sad and depressing, even embarrassing at times (for me that is). I am here to tell you that in spite of the hard times you too can learn to be happy with who you are, if you just trust in the Lord our God.

As another disclaimer, I would like to say that I do not condone divorce. I am not telling you to seek out a life without your husband or wife, but we all know that it is not always our choice.

Divorce can happen for many different reasons, and each and every reason is devastating to all parties involved. There are times that staying with someone may be harmful to you and to your children. When your spouse is hurting you and/or your children, it is not only physically damaging, but it is also psychologically damaging. It sounds like the easiest reason for divorce, but it is actually very hard for the victims of abuse to leave their spouse. However, it can be accomplished.

There are times that your spouse just doesn't want to work it out. No matter how hard you try to make the marriage work, the other party in the marriage has committed to the divorce.

There are so many different scenarios that preclude divorce. It is not my goal to speak about divorce. It is not my goal to help you determine if it is the right thing for you and your family. I am here to talk about life after divorce when there are no other options.

Ladies and gentlemen, you are now divorced. You are lonely, you are scared, and you are feeling desperate about your future. I know because I have been there. There are so many different emotions that bombard you all at once. Often times you feel like you have failed in your marriage. You have failed as a parent because you are now a single parent.

Well, *stop it*! You don't need to beat yourself up. It is what you do next that will define whether or not you are a failure. Your marriage may not have worked, but you can still have a very successful life for you, your children, and even your ex-spouse.

Some of you seek out the first person you find and marry them. They are nice to you, and they show you interest. After all who else is going to come along to fill that lonely void in your life. Having someone is better than having no one. Right? Wrong!

Others will find themselves bringing someone home different with them often, searching for that perfect someone. You go out to the bars even if that is not your scene and pick up every Tom, Dick, and Harry looking for Mr. Right. I get it; this is the desperate feeling that I was talking about. You feel like if you don't find someone now, even if that person is not someone you are in love with, at least it is someone, and you won't be alone. This is a dangerous route to take, for you and for your children. Not only does it often time lead to substance abuse and diseases, but it is also psychologically damaging to you and your children.

You deserve better; you deserve to find someone that you love and that will love you back unconditionally. It is okay to be alone; in fact, you might find you like it. I know it is hard to believe, but it is true.

Also, I want you to remember something or rather someone, your children. There is an epidemic in our country today, and that is grandparents raising their grandchildren because parents turn to drugs and alcohol or they just decide that they do not want to be parents any longer. This is completely unacceptable.

Grandparents have already done their job as parents. They put in their time and effort raising you; they need to be able to relax for the remainder of their lives instead of cleaning up your mess. Even though the children are lucky they have someone to love them, there is always going to be this empty abandoned feeling that follows them the rest of their lives. Too many times I have seen the pain in children's eyes when their parents have abandoned them to a life of substance abuse or illegal practices.

We have a saying in my line of work, which we will discuss later, "Behavior is a form of communication." Children act out in many different forms. Some become very difficult to deal with in and out of school and end up on several different kinds of medication. Some turn to their own promiscuity and often times ends up pregnant before they leave high school. Other times they turn to substance abuse and illegal practices themselves.

Your children don't deserve to experience any one of these scenarios. What they deserve is your unconditional love and support. Sorry, but their needs come first at this point. That doesn't mean that you have to give up on your own needs; you just have to learn some balance.

As I stated, you can have a loving, successful life for you, you're children, and even your ex. Even though things didn't work out for you and your spouse, you can still learn to be partners in raising your children. Forgiveness is the key. I know that your ex has hurt you, and it feels better to hate them for the things they have done to you, but trust me when I say forgiveness really does feel better. Your children need to see a unified team that is raising them. Think about how much they are hurting every time you bad mouth the father or mother. They love both of you, and they need both of you. Set aside your differences, and learn to forgive each other for the many hurtful things that have occurred in your marriage. You might find that you and your ex. become very good friends, even though the marriage didn't work out.

This book isn't just about women and men who have gone through divorce; it is also about making the most of your life as a single person. You may not have ever been married or your spouse may have gone home to be with the Lord. This book is about how to make the most out of your life and finding the person God meant for you to be.

I am going to take you on my journey as a single woman and a single parent with the hope that you will acquire the ability to look within yourself and find happiness with who you are as a person.

> If you forgive those who sin against you, your heavenly father will forgive you. But if you refuse to forgive others, your Father will not forgive your sins. (Matthew 6:14–15 NLT)

Now on to my story. As I stated, I have been divorced for twenty-two years. I was so young when I divorced. I had no idea what to do or how to do it. I remember sitting in my apartment looking at my babies wondering what to do next. I knew that I needed to get a job. Up until that point, I was a stay-at-home mother. To get a job, I needed a babysitter, but I had no money to pay a babysitter. It seemed like an endless cycle that I wasn't sure how to get around. So I started babysitting other children for a short time. The next several years were a blur of odd jobs just trying to make ends meet. I finally moved back to my hometown where my mother helped me a great deal.

Frankly, for many years, I was still just maintaining, waiting for life to happen, waiting for the perfect man, waiting for the perfect job, waiting for the perfect house. Well, you get the picture—always waiting, always waiting for someone else to take control of my life. It never occurred to me that I needed to make my own way, to get out there and make things happen. After all, I had two children to raise; living day to day, pay check to pay check was all I knew.

I had no idea that there was more to life, that there was more available to me. For years, my life was status quo: go to work and take care of my children, nothing more. The only thing I was truly proud of was that I always put my children's needs first. I just didn't know how to balance my needs with my children's needs. I thought that I needed someone else to do that for me.

I thought if only I had a man to take care of me, he would be my salvation, the answer to my prayers. He would take the desperate feel of survival away. He would take the hurt away. He would take the lonely away. I was always looking for that perfect someone to live my life for me. I just knew he was right around the next corner though I was not actively going to seek him out. My children deserved more than that; they deserved to have their physical and emotional needs to be met before my own.

God was always with me, regardless of what was going on in my life. Here is a story that shows how truly awesome he is. Through this time of trying to find myself, I took a job at a local convenience store. The boys were still very young. In the year 1998, on a Saturday (my first day out of training), I was robbed at gunpoint. I will never forget a moment of this event.

There was a lull in customers, so I went to stock the cooler. I noticed a man come in, so I went to the front to wait for him to pay. He came up behind me and put a gun in my stomach, demanding the money. The gas pumps started to fill up. He told me to wait on them and not say anything or he would start shooting. I took the opportunity to turn and look at him, with the excuse of telling him that someone would notice if I didn't have any money to make change. He gave me a little back to put in the register. I waited on several customers. I was shaking and crying the entire time, and not one person paid attention. After it cleared out a little, he took me to the back with the gun in my back. I looked over, and two couples looked at me and rushed out of the store. They never reported that something was going on to the police. In the back room, he shoved me against the wall while getting the security tape. He then put a bandana around my neck and tried to strangle me. I was silently praying the entire time. He suddenly let go and left. I fell to the floor and then crawled out into the store where people rushed to help me. The man was eventually caught and did time in jail.

The part of the story that is a miracle, if you will, is what happened exactly one week prior to the robbery. I was still in training, when God sent me a message. A man came in to pay for his gas. He handed me a credit card but didn't let go when he handed it to me. While we were both holding his credit card, he looked me in the eye and said, "You are about to go through some hard times, but don't worry because God will help you through it." I wasn't sure what to make of it at the time, but after the robbery, I knew that God had sent me a message that he was going to be there with me through the robbery.

It took me a long time to realize that he was always there, whether it was through a robbery, if it was financial, or in trying to find love.

Finally one day, in the fall of 2000, I met a man, *not* the perfect man, definitely *not* the right man, but I did get one important thing from this relationship, the love of teaching. I didn't fall in love with him, but I did fall in love with his profession. He was a fourth grade teacher, and I spent a lot of time in his classroom helping him. I helped grade papers, I helped make bulletin boards, and I even helped with lesson planning. I started volunteering at the school helping students that struggled. It still never occurred to me that I could be a teacher. After all, I was a divorced, single parent, and college dropout.

One day another teacher in the building approached me and told me that I should go back to school to become a teacher. She told me I was a natural and that my place was in the classroom. Frankly, I was floored; I had no idea that was even in the realm of possibilities.

I started thinking about it. *Could I really do this? Was I smart enough to be a teacher? Would I be any good at it? Did I have enough money?* The questions were endless.

So I did the only thing that I could do; I hit my knees, praying about what God wanted for me. I wasn't even sure what exactly I wanted; all I knew was when I was helping out in the classroom, it just felt right. I knew that I loved working with children. I loved helping them learn and be successful.

I asked God to put up road blocks in my way if he did not want me to jump into this new endeavor. He not only opened all doors for me, he escorted me through. Who was I to doubt God and not walk through when he offered his hand?

I went on to get a bachelor of science in elementary education and special education in 2004. I also have my masters of education for elementary administration and special education administration and a specialist degree for educational administration.

I started my career as a special education teacher in a special education classroom working at the middle school level and then went on to work at the high school as well. I was then given a job working as a process coordinator. As a process coordinator, I oversee junior high and high school special education.

I put myself out there, and it paid off. This was the beginning of my journey to living life to the fullest.

I won't lie to you; it was not always an easy road. There were days that, if I stopped and thought about all that was piled on my already full plate, I may have had a nervous breakdown. Most of the time while working on my bachelor's degree, I had two and three jobs and pulling eighteen to twenty credit hours at school each semester. I survived, mostly on autopilot. If I had thought about what I was doing, I probably would have become extremely overwhelmed.

I tried to set aside time to spend with my children, but that wasn't always easy. I had to keep telling myself that this endeavor was not only about improving my future but also theirs. The boys were in the fourth and fifth grade when I started back to school.

My oldest was always so mature and caring. He has a sense of humor that can always put a smile on my face. When I am upset or angry, he can always make me laugh and bring me out of my mood. He has a gift with words; I am always trying to get him to write because when he does, it is very difficult to put down his work. My youngest is fourteen months younger, loving and full of energy. He has always been a sense of comfort for me. He is very smart; he has a gift of knowledge. He just seems to know how to work out any kind of problem, whether it is logical or mechanical. He was one of those children that were always taking apart things to see how it worked. Thank goodness he was always able to put them back together, and they still work.

My youngest was always the one inclined to give me gray hair because he was always hurting himself doing something crazy. Although they both tried hard at times to give me gray hair, by doing things such as jump off my roof onto the trampoline. Both boys were very independent and full of life.

They both supported my decision to go back to school, well most of the time anyway. They didn't always understand why I had to work so hard. They didn't always understand why I was choosing a career that didn't pay much. In the end, I think they were proud of my hard work.

My youngest son would often sit on my lap while I was working on the computer or studying. One time he was down at the creek, a couple blocks from the house, fishing with one of his buddies. He had been trying for weeks to catch this catfish that was for all intents and purposes his Moby Dick.

One afternoon while I was taking a timed test on the computer, he came running in with his catfish in his hand grinning from ear to ear, yelling, "I got him, Mom, I got him!" I couldn't walk away from the test but was torn by wanting to help and congratulate him. I hollered for his brother to get him something to put the fish in, while I quickly finished my test. I can't remember what I got on the test, but I will never forget the look on his face while holding his fish high in the air. Of course we had to take the fish down to the local newspaper so he could get his picture taken with the fish to put in the next edition of the paper.

I learned to cherish each and every one of these special moments with my children. Time goes by so quickly that every moment with them is important. I made time for their ball games and science fairs. I tried to balance my time with them and my time I needed to commit to school.

Every minute of the day was very important. I took my books with me everywhere so I wouldn't miss a single minute of the day that could be spent with my children. I studied while sitting at basketball practice. I studied in the car waiting to pick them up from school. I even studied in the drive-through at McDonalds.

I won't ever say I was a perfect parent. I made plenty of mistakes along the way, but I loved them every step of the way. I tried to always put their needs, their wants, and their desires before my own.

> Children are a gift from the Lord; they are a reward from him. (Psalms 127:3 NLT)

Making the grades and spending time with my children weren't the only difficult aspects of this excursion. Money was a colossal mountain that was always looming in the near distance. There never seemed to be enough money. I heard more from creditors than I did from family.

Money was probably the hardest part about taking this journey. I was poor before I started back to school, but it was nothing like what I went through after starting school. Yes, there were Pell grants, scholarships, and student loans. Oh how I wish I had not taken out those student loans, but at that time, it was a necessary evil. As I previously stated, there were times that I held down two and even three different jobs just to get enough work to make a living.

Then there is my credit score; I am not ashamed of my credit score. I will tell you that at one point, my credit score hit rock bottom, but I did what I had to in order to survive. There were many times that I would dig through the couch looking for spare change to buy a loaf of bread to feed my children. We ate a lot of pasta and potatoes because they were cheap foods that would fill the endless stomachs of my ever-growing boys. The boys knew that we did not have a lot of money, but I tried to hide exactly how poor we really were. I tried to get them what I could, when I could get it.

If you have ever studied Ruby Payne, you will know what I am talking about when I say that I had developed a Ruby Payne mentality. Whenever there was anything offered free, I was all about it. When I received a little bit of money, I didn't spend it appropriately. I would try to buy something for the boys because there may not be another chance to get them something special. When there was extra food, I would gorge myself, because I never knew when I may not have any food.

Between the lack of money, the stress of the hard work, and the depression, I started to pack on the pounds. Yes, I said depression; it was hard not to slip into depression. Think about it; I had no money, I was constantly working, and it had been a long time since anyone found me attractive let alone love me.

I gained weight pretty quickly mostly due to depression. The more depressed I became, the fatter I became, thus creating a cycle. Depression led to weight gain, weight gain led to depression.

There were many nights I cried myself to sleep, many nights I wanted to throw in the towel and call it quits. I felt like I was drowning; the weight on my chest was unbearable. No matter how hard I swam, the surfs of the water was always out of reach. When I was alone, there were times I would scream out to God to take it all away. I know that he was there; I could feel him holding me up, soothing my tormented heart. Even though he was there with me, my troubles were too.

No matter how depressed I got, there was a part of me that knew that my children and family depended on me. My children did not deserve to live a life without their mother. They did not deserve to feel the pains of abandonment and loss. My children's needs came before my own, so I continued to push forward.

More importantly, God had given me life, and who was I to throw it away? Who was I to spit in the face of God and all that he had given me?

A lot of people didn't realize how depressed I had become. I got pretty good at hiding behind a mask, a mask of silliness mostly. I have always been a rather goofy person. My mother often stated that I act just like Lucille Ball. You have to be able to laugh at yourself; have a little fun.

Anyway I digress. I think you get the point; this journey was not an easy one. God never promised it would be an easy journey, but he did promise to be there holding me in his arms throughout the journey. He also promised not to give me anything that I couldn't handle. Although there were times I would scream out, "I can't handle anymore!" Somehow even though I said I couldn't handle things, I ended up coming out a better person in the end. I am here to tell you that I would not change a minute of this journey I call my life because now I am taking control of my life and not letting it control me.

> Do not be afraid or discouraged, for the Lord is the one who goes before you. He will be with you; he will neither fail you nor forsake you. (Deuteronomy 31:8 NLT)

Now that we have the sad, depressing part out of the way, I can get on with the rest of the story. By the way, I would not change one minute of that part of my life because it is what helped to shape the person that I am today.

So get off of the couch feeling sorry for yourself because of what life has dwelt you, and get out there and start making your life happen. I'm not saying that going back to school is the route you should take. I am just saying take some time to figure out what is right for you and don't forget to include God in that decision making process. He will lead you to places you never thought possible; he is the one that truly knows your heart. It is not going to happen all at once; take one day at a time. Just remember, God will be there for you if you just let him. He will give you the strength you never knew you had in you. You don't need anyone or anything; *God* is the only thing you need. So have a little faith and start living.

SILLY MOMENT

One afternoon after church, we went out to a local restaurant to eat lunch. There were a few families at the table, probably fifteen or so people in attendance. I was at one end of the table and my nephew, Jacob, was at the other. My family has several inside jokes that we like to laugh about. On this particular day, my nephew made a gesture from the other side of the table that caused me to laugh hysterically. While I was laughing, my head went back and then forward. This would have been fine except as I went forward, my straw went straight up my nose and stuck there, causing everyone else at the table to laugh hysterically. Blood was running down my nose as I removed the straw, but I still could not stop laughing. This story is brought up often among family and friends. "Only to Lena" is what usually follows this story and many of the other stories of things have that I done.

FINDING MY PASSION

Even though I found my dream job, this was only the beginning. I still hadn't figured out how to live life to the fullest. I poured my heart and soul into raising my children and my job, but my life was still lacking. Don't get me wrong; this was a great start and very rewarding. I have two wonderful boys. Well, they are now young men just starting their own adventures of life. Also, I love working in the world of education. I am truly a lifelong learner, but there was still something missing.

I don't know if it was a midlife crisis or what, but I felt like life was still passing me by; there was still so much to see and do. I didn't want to miss out on anything this life has to offer. Well, let's face it; there are no do-overs in life. I'm sure we would all like to go back to our twenties and do a lot of things differently, but that is just not an option.

Then one day, I realized what I was missing, how to enjoy life. I was working so hard at everything, but I was not enjoying myself. I was happy, but I was not having fun in life. I didn't know how to let loose and do something just for fun.

So I set out to find what it was that I enjoy doing for fun. I really started thinking about what it was that I have always wanted to do. What I came up with felt like the impossible. Honestly, it took me a couple of years to make my way down this next path of my adventure.

Are you curious yet as to what I came up with? The answer is travel. I have always wanted to travel, to see what the world has to offer. I don't mean hop in a plane and fly to another part of the country and stay in a beautiful hotel or condo; don't get me wrong, that is great too. No, I have always wanted to get in a car and drive across the country and experience all that this wonderful country has to offer. I wanted to see all of the magnificence that God created, meet people, and experience different cultures that make up the melting pot we call America.

The problem is I was still single, and there was no one to go with me, which is why it took me so long to fulfill this part of my journey. Everyone knows you can't take a vacation alone. Right? Once again, I was playing the waiting game. I waited and waited for a man to show up in my life so that I could start having fun.

I am not sure how it happened, but one day, it struck me like a blow to the head. *Why do I have to wait for a man to go with me? I am a strong, independent woman that can do anything I set my mind to.* Guess what? So are you; all you have to do is have a little faith that God will give you the tools and the courage you need to be able to fulfill anything you set out to do.

So that is what I did; I started planning my first trip that took place in 2008. Yes, I said first because I have gone every year since. And yes, I went by myself. Well, almost by myself, my dog Max went with me. Max is my golden retriever and my best friend.

I am going to take you through this adventure with me. Some of it may be fun, some a little quirky, maybe some scary parts, and, as I stated before, even some embarrassing parts. I will try not to embarrass you too much, but I can't promise anything.

One of the best parts about taking a trip is the planning aspect. I wanted to be ready for anything and everything. For those that know me, they can tell you how obsessive compulsive I can be; I planned this trip down to the minute detail. I bought camping gear, clothes, shoes, food, maps, etcetera. I spent hours on the computer researching the best routes to take and camp grounds to stay. You got to love Google maps, that street view is awesome. I even calculated exactly how much money I would need, how many miles it would take, and how much gas I would need. I had every scenario planned so that I would be prepared for anything that might happen.

I was ready for any danger that might come my way. I do not and will not ever carry a gun. Dereck Price, a friend of mine, is always bugging me about taking a gun on these trips. Even though I won't carry a gun, there are alternatives that come in quite handy. One necessity is a can of wasp spray. It works as well as pepper spray but can shoot much farther. The only weapon that I carry is a knife. In fact, I have knives stashed all over my car and on my purse. My mother laughs at me because the knife I carry on my purse is not very big, only a couple of inches long. The thing is, I don't want to hurt anyone unless absolutely necessary. Trust me, I know exactly where to use that knife should I need to. It may not be long, but the places I will put it, the length will not matter.

I have also taken self-defense classes. I want to have fun, but I also want to be safe. This is one reason I sleep in my car as opposed to a tent. I always have a tent just in case, but I prefer the car. After all, I am a single woman out there by myself. This way, I can lock myself in while I am sleeping.

> I will lie down in peace and sleep, for you alone, O Lord, will keep me safe. (Psalms 4:8 NLT)

Every year, I have fine-tuned how to maximize the packing of the car. I had a Jeep Grand Cherokee for this first trip. I started off trying to tie a bunch of stuff to the top of the car and wrap it with tarps. Very redneck, I know. I even made it all the way to Montana that way. That's when it started raining, and all of my things were getting soaked. I managed to get everything I need inside the car now. I put all of the seats down in the back of my SUV. The passenger side of the car holds the cooler, food box, luggage, etcetera. Max, my dog, stays on the driver's side of the car. At night, I sleep on the driver's side, and Max sleeps at my feet.

Another thing I did that evolved throughout the years was what I call redneck screens. I bought screen from the local hardware store and cut it to fit my car windows. I then duck-taped it to the inside of the car so that I could roll down my windows at night. I felt safer, and it kept the bugs out while letting in a breeze. I also duck-taped the entire door where Max sat to preserve the plastic on the door from being scratched.

I also worried about Max getting too warm in the back, so I bought battery-powered pans that I bungeed to the back of the front seats. That way, if I needed to leave Max in the car for a few minutes, I wouldn't worry so much. I would just leave the windows down (with the screens) and turn on the fans for him. I would also leave him a fresh bowl of water. That being said, I still didn't leave him for more than a few minutes and not at all in the warm climates.

Making sure Max was secure and comfortable was very important to me. I have his leash hooked to the back of the car so that he can only get to the back of the driver's seat. I had to do this because he would have tried to sit on my lap the entire trip, and well Max is a golden retriever and would simply not fit on my lap.

As you can see, Max gets a little anxious in the car. In fact, he gets anxious whenever he doesn't have me in his line of vision. My sister swears that he is the biggest wimp of a dog she has ever seen. She may be correct; whenever he gets nervous, he usually gets behind me and pokes his head out from between my legs to see what is going on. I will let you be the judge of how wimpy Max is as we go through my story.

Other than needing to be right by me throughout the trip and whining every time we come to a stop sign, Max does a great job on these trips. Having Max with me really is like having another person along. Even better at times, I talked to him throughout the trip, and he never once gave me any grief by talking back.

Now I was prepared with all my lists, supplies, weapons, and classes. I had everything I needed and was ready to take off on my first trip.

Needless to say, I was completely terrified to actually take off. It didn't help that everyone I talked to couldn't believe I was taking such risks. They told me every horror story imaginable, but I would not be swayed. I was bound and determined to follow through with my plans.

The first thing I had to do was figure out where I wanted to go for my trek across country. I knew I didn't want to go someplace close. I don't know if I told you this previously, but I am an avid reader. My book of choice at the time was the *Twilight* series. Yes, it is true. I am a Twilight Mom! Actually a Twilight teacher! To clarify, several teachers in one of the elementary schools in my district went nuts over the series. We have a great time with lots of bonding over the books and movies.

So I picked Forks, Washington, as my destination. Now I wasn't going to Forks because of the books per say, but Stephanie Meyers made it sound like such a beautiful place, I decided that Forks should be my journey's end. Little did I know, the entire journey would be absolutely magnificent!

I suppose I should tell you where I am from so that you will see the gravity of how far I went on this trip alone. I am from southwest Missouri, very near Joplin. The start of my route went north through Kansas City and then on to South Dakota where I caught I-90 going west. My first stop was pretty uneventful, which is good because I may have turned right around and gone home had it not been. I really enjoyed going across South Dakota; it really is not much to see except miles and miles of grassland. It was so new to me, and I loved every minute of it. The landscape is so different than Missouri. Many parts of South Dakota is what I lovingly refer to as bumpy. If you look off to your right or left, you will see what looks like an ocean of bumpy grassland covered with a very fragrant yellow flower. There would be grass everywhere, and then suddenly, a small, little pond would spring up in the middle of the grass.

As you are driving along I-90, you start seeing one sign after another for miles and miles for a place called Wall Drug in Wall, South Dakota. It sits just on the edge of the Badlands, a great place to stop and get a bite to eat and some souvenirs. It is hard not to want to stop and see what all of the fuss is about.

There was another place that I passed that I stopped on the way back home; it is called 1880 Town. This was a really neat place to stop. When I stopped, it was sweat drenching hot, and I did not want to leave Max in the car. I went up to the main building just to check it out, where I explained my situation with Max. After telling me they let dogs come through, I hurriedly went back to get Max. This was a refreshing concept to me. I loved being able to meander down the main street of 1880 Town with Max.

This town, or I guess I should say museum, was designed with the appearance of a working town set in the 1880s. As you walk into the different buildings, you feel as if the proprietors had just walked out the door and would be back shortly.

This quaint little town had everything a town needs from the local bank to the church at the end of the street. You could even stop and get a scoop of ice cream in the saloon. If you are so inclined, you can also rent period dress and walk around in costume. There was a road leading out of town to a homestead about a quarter mile down the road. I felt just like Laura Ingalls Wilder walking home from school. The town offers much more than I could ever describe. Stop and see for yourself.

After leaving South Dakota, I caught Highway 212 that was a two-lane highway that cut across Wyoming and on into Montana. I can't remember exactly where I was at, but shortly after I got onto Highway 212, I hit some serious road construction. When I say serious, I mean that I was stopped for forty-five minutes waiting to get through. Everyone was out of their car standing and waiting. I had Max out to stretch his legs. Seriously, I have never had to wait that long for road construction. It was well worth the wait; it was a fantastic drive, rolling hills that gradually got bigger and bigger until I thought I was in the mountains. Oh boy, was I wrong. I soon found out what a real mountain looks like. The mountains in Montana were magnificent creations of God.

I came across a gas station along the road side. I got the most mouthwatering taffy I have every eaten. I visited with a few of the locals while I was there. They were a good bunch of people. This is one of the things I love most about my trips around the country: talking to the locals and learning the different cultures. This was so different than all of the horror stories that people told me, trying to convince me not to go on this trip. In fact, in all of my trips, I have found that people all over are very friendly and even protective of me when they find out that I travel alone.

As I was driving along I-90 through Montana and Idaho, another couple traveling the same route I was on would stop and visit with me at every rest area. The woman would tell me how frustrated she would get if another traveler would get to close to me or looked like they were cutting me off. I spent most of a day traveling along with this very nice couple.

Another instance where I found very nice people was my first night in Washington, and I had stayed at a state park. It was my first night of camping that I actually built a fire. I had already camped two other nights but had not built a fire yet. I just used my camping stove and made do. Now, mind you, I was still very green at the whole camping by myself. I didn't know that you couldn't pick up wood around the campsite to make your fire. There were signs all over telling you not to pick up the wood. I didn't know that I was supposed to buy it before I had arrived. It was getting late, and the state camp ground was packed full of people. In fact I was shocked at the number of campers. This is not my ideal way to camp; I like to be off by myself as much as possible. I set up my camp stove to cook dinner, but it was a little chilly, and I wanted a fire.

This is when I learned the generosity of others was still alive and well. There was a couple in the campsite across from me that seemed pleasant. They were sitting by their fire drinking a glass of wine. I approached them and asked if they sold wood at the entrance of the campground. They were unsure, and I told them that it was okay because I had my stove, and it was not a problem. I thanked them for their time and was on my way.

A short time later the gentleman walked over with an arm load of wood and some paper. He said they had plenty and proceeded to start a fire for me.

This was not what I had expected. It was such a nice thing for someone to do. I was so moved by their kindness; they will never know what that meant to me. It was not that I needed a fire; it was that they had such giving hearts.

You will see other acts throughout my story of the kindness of others, the friendship they so easily offered to a stranger. This alone touched my heart in a way that I never expected and is the reason that I continue to travel each year.

There were a lot of people that would stop and talk to me through all of my journeys, some very nice and then some that I tried to steer clear. There was one rest area I stopped; I'm not sure which state I was in at the time that stuck in my memory. I had been walking Max when a woman stopped me and asked if she could pet my dog. I appreciated the gesture of asking and let her pet Max. She was very friendly as we talked about dogs and our love of them. A few moments later, her husband walked up to stand next to her. Max instantly crouched down with a low growl and slowly backed away from the man. I was shocked; I had never heard Max growl at anyone. He had never acted this way period, so I took his cue and politely said my good-byes. I quickly but nonchalantly got back into my car locking the door. There may not have been a thing wrong with this gentleman, but animals can sense things that we can't sense, and I trust Max completely.

> God made all sorts of wild animals, livestock, and small animals, each able to reproduce more of its own kind. And God saw that it was good. (Genesis 1:25 NLT)

I had so many memories in rest areas, probably because I stopped at almost every rest area on the trip. I did this so that Max and I could get out and stretch our legs. This trip wasn't about speed; it was about the experiences. Washington had some great rest areas. At one, I had to just laugh; people can be so funny. There were seagulls everywhere and a sign that said not to feed them. The funny part is all of the people standing right next to the sign were feeding the birds.

Another rest area in Washington had a great walking trail through the woods. Now I know that it was probably not the brightest thing for me to go walking in the woods at a rest area, but I just couldn't help myself. If it makes you feel any better, I am the type of person that when I travel, I am very observant about what is going on around me. I am also observant about what God is trying to tell me. If he says it is not a place I need to be, then I don't stick around. I didn't feel anything out of place at the time, so I took a little hike through the woods with Max. Hiking is one of my favorite pastimes, how could I pass up this pretty little hike?

The eastern side of Washington was not really what I had expected. It was very flat, brown, and dry. I saw several dust devils off in the fields. I was a little disappointed at first until shortly past George, Washington, when I decided to pull off on a scenic overlook. I was so glad I stopped.

After this stop, the scenery changed dramatically. It went from brown and flat to green trees in the mountains. Washington definitely has a diverse landscape.

While planning my route, I was very careful to plan around taking a ferry. I had never been on a ferry and was a bit weary to try. The only place that I might come across a ferry was in the Seattle area. So I planned my route to go all the way down and around to the south of Seattle and then back north to finally catch Highway 101 to go around the Olympic National Park. In the meantime, I had to cross the Hood Canal Bridge. I almost panicked when detour signs started popping up. I got lucky; the bridge wasn't closing down for another week.

I was so excited when I finally made it onto Highway 101 because that meant that I was almost there. I had to go through a quaint little town called Port Angeles. I remember thinking, *This is some place I would like to live.*

For all of you Twilight fans, there were several stores to buy memorabilia in Port Angeles and Forks. I just had to stop in and get my dear friend Lea Ann a Twilight souvenir while I was in the neighborhood.

Finally, I made it to Forks, Washington, on my fourth day. I had camped all the way thus far. I knew that I wanted to stay in a motel to recoup before heading into the Olympic National Park. I could not check into the motel for a couple of hours, so I went sightseeing around Forks. That took me about five minutes. Forks, Washington, was not a large town at all, but they had several Twilight stores that were packed full of fans. We spent the rest of the time in a quiet, little park on the edge of town called Tillicum Park. I also learned while driving around Forks that I could buy a shower for three dollars at one of the other motels. That definitely came in handy after camping in the Olympic National Park.

Max and I spent the night recouping before the rest of our camping excursion. As I was watching the news that night, there was a story about a man and his daughter getting mauled by a black bear in the Glacier National Park. *Great, now I was really nervous about camping by myself.*

There were so many different campgrounds that I could have chosen in the Olympic National Park. I chose to camp in the Hoh Rainforest and was not disappointed. Before coming to Washington, I did not know there were so many different shades of green.

The drive to the campground was twelve miles down a remote road under the cover of trees. About halfway to the campground was a little gift shop in the middle of nowhere. It seemed crazy out there with nothing else around. I stopped and bought my family souvenirs. I explained to the clerk how nervous I was about camping because I had just heard about the family being mauled by the bear. She told me not to be nervous but be cautious. She also told me I needed a bear bell, which is exactly that, a bell you hook to your belt. Supposedly bears mostly go the opposite direction when they hear noise. Believe it or not, this helped me relax.

As I stated previously, I like to feel like I am off and away from everyone else when I camp. The Hoh campground was perfect. The campsites were not right on top of one another. I even had two elk wander through my campsite. I set up my tent for the first time. I was staying for a couple of days and wanted to be able to stretch out. Once I picked out my site, I got busy setting up camp. I am sure that if anyone saw me, they probably would have thought that I was a few bricks short of a load. I was walking around my campsite with the biggest grin on my face. I jumped from one log to the next just celebrating. See how liberating it is to be single; you can act as crazy as you want, and no one cares.

As I was jumping the logs, I noticed the biggest slug I have ever seen in my life. I swear it looked like an army helmet. I poked and prodded it, but it was sucked right onto the log. Finally, I gave up and decided to go for a walk in the woods. After securing Max, because he wasn't allowed in the back country, I went exploring. A few yards through the woods behind my campsite, I found the Hoh River. I walked along it for a while and then back into the woods. As I was walking, I got a phone call from my son, Jordan. Jordan was taking care of my two cats and had some bad news for me. My sweet little sissy cat had passed away. I remember sitting down on the nearest fallen tree and crying in the middle of the woods by myself. It was very sad, but I had to put it aside for now and get back to camp. Max would be getting anxious about my whereabouts.

My Boys; truly a gift from God!

This is how I slept at night.

This is how Max sat for most of the trip.

The quaint little town of 1880 Town.

I don't know what was more beautiful; Montana's landscape or the wide open sky.

The funny things you see at rest areas. There was a sign stating not to feed the sea gulls and right next to the sign were two women feeding the sea gulls.

Spectacular view of the Columbia River in Washington State

The actual Forks High School for all of you Twilight fans.

A replica of Bella's truck at the visitor's information center in Forks, WA

Campground in the Hoh Rainforest

Max lounging by the tent in the Hoh Rainforest campground

You Twilight fans will understand this reference.
I thought it was hysterical when I came upon
this sign, so I just had to take a picture.

First Beach in La Push, WA on a rainy afternoon

One of those crazy interesting things you see while traveling. I just love the pull along!

What do you think? Is it a bear???

The Adirondack Mountains in upstate
New York is just breath taking.

These old tombstones were in my campsite in Mount
Desert Island in Maine. You try sleeping!!

Rugged splendor of the Badlands in South Dakota

A peak- a- boo of the ocean in Cape Blanco campground in Oregon.

Camping amongst the towering pines in Oregon is an amazing experience.

These are made out of Redwood trees. How cool is that!

The towering red rocks of Utah

The Grand Canyon in its overwhelming
display of God's magnificent artwork.

My second day in the Hoh Rainforest I planned to go hiking. There were a couple of shorter trails and then a really long trail. I knew that I couldn't go on the long one since I had Max back at the car. The temperature was no more than sixty-five degrees, and I felt very comfortable letting Max stay in the car with the windows down. He had his food and water and was secured in the car with his sleeping bag. He laid right down for his morning nap.

I knew that I was only going to hike on the two shorter trails, but I was going to be prepared for anything that might happen. I had my backpack that was stocked full of survival gear. I had my bear bell securely attached to my belt as I set off for my hike. There were several people milling around at the trail head. I didn't pay them much mind as I started off. My bear bell was working quite well; it was loud! I tried to put the noise out of my head until I started noticing who all was on the trail with me, mostly older couples. Here I was all geared up for the worst to happen, and I am walking with a bunch of retired people on an afternoon stroll. I felt so silly, I tried to duck behind a tree and at least take my bell off and hide it away in my backpack. I figured that if these people could survive on the trail, I probably could as well. I put my embarrassment out of my head and concentrated on the grandeur around me. This was not like any forest I had ever been in.

I read all of the signs posted trying to learn all I could about the forest. When a tree falls in the forest, other saplings feed off the tree causing a truly spectacular sight. The intricate balance of the forest has so much to teach us about life. God put us all on the earth to work together and learn from one another to survive along the path that God led us down. We all have gifts and talents that we can bring forth to help society prosper. My gifts may not be the same as yours, but each and every one is important to the balance of life. We are all significant just like the fallen tree in the forest.

> I am leaving you with a gift—peace of mind and heart. And the peace I give isn't like the peace the world gives. So don't be troubled or afraid. (John 14:27 NLT)

After a two-night stay in the Hoh Rainforest campground, I made my way back to Forks. The campground didn't have a shower, and I could only go so long on sponge baths. There was a shower calling my name. At one of the motels in Forks, you could buy a shower for three dollars. It was nice to feel fresh and revived before heading out again.

It was cool and rainy as I headed toward La Push. I figured since I was that close, I had to check it out. You Twilight fans will understand. In the book, the vampires were not allowed passed a certain point because it was wolf territory. On my way to La Push, I came across this sign that said "No Vampires Beyond This Point." I thought it was hilarious, so I had to take a picture. La Push wasn't very big, but it was an appealing little town right on the ocean. It was raining, but that didn't stop me from taking pictures on First Beach. The rain was coming off the ocean right in my face. I could not see what I was taking pictures of; I just pointed and clicked. I was lucky the pictures came out as good as they did.

There were a couple other beaches that you could get to just outside of La Push. I really wanted to check it out, but you had to hike a little ways to get to the beach, and it just wasn't worth it in the rain. So I decided to head back toward home. On this trip, I was driving back the same way that I had come.

On the way home, I can't remember exactly where I was at the time, but I was getting pretty tired. I love to drive, but fourteen eight-hour days of traveling can start to get a little boring.

Now I am the type of person that doesn't usually get bored. I am easily entertained, and this was one of those times that I decided it was time to entertain myself.

So I passed the time by talking aloud. I was talking to Max in the thickest, deep south accent. Now, I wasn't talking about anything in particular; I was just a chatty Kathy. I was telling Max about the sites that we passed, about the weather outside, about the things that we had done on the trip. Well, you get the idea. I was talking nonsense. I told you how goofy I can be.

Anyway, I pulled off to get gas, and a gentleman pumping his gas at the pump opposite of me commented on my beautiful dog. Seemed to be a very nice gentlemen, but I will remind you that I had been talking nonstop with this deep south accent in the car. I replied to this lovely gentleman in the same silly accent, "Why I thank ya kindly, my good sir. Have yourself a lovely day."

I realized what I had done, when it looked like the poor man had a coronary right there beside his car. I thought his mouth was never going to shut as he stammered some kind of reply as he got back into his car. I can't say exactly what was going through his mind, but I am pretty sure he thought I was completely insane.

The only somewhat bad experience I had throughout my first trip was on my way home. I was somewhere in Iowa, and I had pushed it hard that day. Max and I were getting tired, but I wanted to get as far as I possibly could before stopping and setting up camp. Typically, I stop around six so that way I have time to set up and get dinner before it gets dark but not on this day. I finally found a roadside campground that looked somewhat decent. The attendant was sitting on the porch as I pulled up. Max immediately started a low growl, and mind you, he is not a dog that growls very often. Remember, this is the dog that when he gets nervous or scared, he hides behind me and pokes his head out from between my legs. I just chalked it up to the fact that I had pushed it too far, and he was tired.

I found my campsite where I backed my car up to a wooded area. I made myself a quick dinner before retiring to my car to sleep. It was only about 10:30 when Max started growling like I had never heard from him. I nudged him and told him that someone was just going to the restroom. This usually settled him right down, but not this time. He was standing up in what I can only explain as an attack stance, and his growling got louder. I tried to sit up to see what was getting him so worked up. To my surprise, there was someone with a flashlight circling around into the woods and up to the backside of my car. There was no reason that this person should be approaching my car from the woods. The person heard Max growling and took off quickly the other way. Max continued to stand over me growling for the next half hour. After that, he lay right on top of me and wouldn't move. I can only assume that he wanted to make sure that I was safe in case he fell asleep. At that moment, I realized that he was not the wimpy dog that everyone thought and he would always protect me.

> God is our refuge and strength, always ready to help in times of trouble. (Psalms 46:1 NLT)

This first trip was by far one of the most rewarding experiences of my entire life. Not only did I experience different cultures and see God's spectacular creations, I was also able to commune with God in a way that I never had before. Originally, I only planned to go on this one trip, but since it left such a mark on my life, I decided to go again the next year. I started planning my next trip as soon as I returned home. Where was the road going to lead me next?

FINDING HUMANITY

My second year to travel, and I was ready. I was so excited to take another trip. I literally planned for the trip from the time I got home from Washington until I left for the next trip a year later. My friends and family will tell you that I drove everyone crazy with my planning. They were so sick and tired of hearing about my plans. I couldn't help myself; the first trip was so monumental that I couldn't wait to hit the road again.

This time around, I really wanted someone to go with me, not because I needed someone but because I wanted someone else to share in the experience. Of course there are not too many people that can take off for about two weeks to make a trip like this. I asked my nephew to go with me because at that time he was the only one that could take off that much time for a trip. I know that it is hard to believe, but he wanted to spend the time with his girlfriend instead. Can't blame him! As it ended up, I went by myself.

Are you excited yet to hear where I decided to take my next journey? My family originates from the northeastern portion of the United States, mostly from Maine. My mother grew up in Maine, and I had always wanted to go back. I love the history of the east coast, so it was decided, that would be my destination.

I wanted to take a bit of a side trip on my way to Maine. My daddy died when I was only three years old. I had not been to his grave in a long time. Daddy was buried in Monroe, Michigan, which is also where I was born.

I also wanted to camp in the Adirondack Mountains. I have always thought that upstate New York was so pretty.

My journey didn't start off too good. It stormed really hard shortly after I entered Indiana. The wind and rain were so hard that I had difficulty staying on the road, so I stopped at a motel for the night.

The next day, not long into the day, I stopped at a rest area. I was approached by what appeared to be a pregnant young woman. She told me that her boyfriend had left her at the rest area with no money and no transportation. She wanted money for a cab to Columbus, Ohio, or in the very least a ride. I told her that I didn't have the money or the room in the car, but I did give her ten dollars to be able to get something to eat. I felt bad, but my gut was telling me to be careful. After she left me, she went over to an older couple and asked them for money as well. I quickly got back in the car and back on the road.

As I stated, I wanted to see my daddy's grave. I was very young when my daddy passed away, and I don't really remember much except through stories my mother told me, but I remember the feel of him. The feeling of warmth and love and security stayed with me long after he had gone home to be with God. I feel as though he is always there with me just as God is always with me.

Even though I was very young when he passed, I still miss him terribly and can't wait until the day I get to see him again.

It had been a long time since I had visited his grave. My sister and I had visited the cemetery several years before but could not find his grave. It was on a Sunday and there was no one around to help us find the grave. We searched for hours trying to locate it, with no avail.

I was so happy that I was able to get help finding his grave this time around. The attendants at the cemetery were very helpful and made me feel like his grave was well taken care of and respected even though we were unable to visit often.

After visiting daddy's grave, I drove around Monroe site seeing my birthplace. I then stopped by the rest area/information center to get some input on campsites. They were very nice and very helpful in finding a place to stay for the night.

It is so funny the things that strike us as interesting. As I was taking Max for a walk, I noticed a motorcycle with the cutest pull along. I had to stop and take a picture. I never said that it took much to entertain me.

After my trip to the cemetery and a drive around town, I found a campsite on Lake Erie. It was kind of cool to camp right on the beach of Lake Erie. I backed my car into the site so that the back of my car opened up to a view of the water.

I had to laugh at Max; he was so funny. Max loves to swim, but where he is used to swimming is calmer waters. Turns out he was scared of the waves coming in on the lake. He would chase them out and then run back as they came in. He would run behind me and poke his head out from between my legs and bark at the waves. It was a very windy day, so there were a lot of waves.

Even though my campsite was right on the beach, this was not my ideal campsite. It was very open, and all of the campers were right next to each other. There was a very nice family that invited me to come over to roast marshmallows and sit by the fire with them.

Later that night, I violated camping etiquette by shining my headlights into practically everyone's campsites. I felt really bad, but it was unavoidable. I unlocked my car with the remote, and it automatically turned on the headlights. It turned night into day for most of the campground.

To make matters worse, I accidentally sounded the panic alarm a short while later. The electronics were messed up on my car, and you had to unlock the car the same way you locked it. For instance, if you used the remote to lock, you had to do the same to unlock. Well, that is how I locked the door, and I had to use the restroom. If I had pulled up the lock on the door, it would have sounded the panic alarm. So I ended up shining the lights over half of the campground and also waking the dead with my panic alarm. Only a few people yelled obscenities at me.

The next morning, I took Max on a long hike before we took off on the road again. It was a beautiful hike on a paved tree-lined trail around the lake. It was very quiet and peaceful; I could have stayed out there all day walking, but alas, I had to get back to driving.

> Do for others what you would like them to do for you. This is a summary of all that is taught in the law and the prophets. (Matthew 7:12 NLT)

I made it all the way to Rochester, New York, before I stopped to camp for the night. As usual, I asked for the most remote campsite. It was a lovely evening, pretty uneventful. My plan for the next day was to make it to my campsite in the Adirondack Mountains, but I didn't quite make it. The next morning, I barely got the car packed before the rain set in. It poured so hard the rain made driving extremely exhausting.

I drove as far as Utica before I finally gave up and found a motel. Waterlogged and tired, I went on the search for food. I found the neatest little pizzeria. I felt like I had stepped into a Godfather movie. The place itself didn't have that appearance, but everyone there was Italian, and they seemed to know each other. The owner was either a boxer at one time or just a huge boxing fan. There were pictures lining the walls of different boxers, and he seemed to be in every one of them. Now I am not a boxing fan, and I really don't know any famous boxers, but I did recognize several of the faces in the pictures. That was really cool! Max and I shared one of the best pizzas I have ever eaten back in the motel room.

The next day, it finally dried out, and I made my way to the campground in the Adirondack Mountains. I stopped at a convenience store on my way to the campground. It was pretty cool outside; I needed to wear a jacket to stay warm. I started up a conversation with the clerk at the store. I had to laugh because she took the whole "one upping someone" to a whole new level. I had commented on how refreshing the cool weather was and that at home it was about 100 degrees. She said that she completely understood because it got to about a 120 in upstate New York all of the time. Now I know that I don't live there to know the weather year around, but really…a 120. There was a woman behind her that looked at me shaking her head no and laughing under her breath.

Going through the Adirondack Mountains was rated as one of the most beautiful drives ever. I pulled over several times to take pictures. There was water, it seemed, at every turn. I stopped at Chapel Pond, which was absolutely breathtaking. I took several pictures, but I didn't really pay close attention to the pictures until I got home. My son, Jordan, asked me what a brown spot was in one of the pictures. I zoomed the camera in to try to get a better look at it. Judge for yourself, but to all of us, it appeared to be a bear up in a tree. Now that is very unsettling that if it were truly a bear, I was in close proximity of this bear and didn't know it. That is scary! Once I had the picture developed, it looked more like a carving than an actual bear. Sigh of relief!

What do you think? Is it a bear?

I wish I had allotted more time to stay at this campground in upstate New York in the Adirondacks, but for the first time on my journeys, I was on a schedule.

I was going to visit my cousin Georgia Bailey and her family in North Berwick, Maine, so I needed to get back on the road.

The drive over to Lake Champlain was nice and pretty uneventful. I stopped at a really neat gift shop and furniture store that specialized in Adirondack chairs. The woman ran the gift shop side, and her husband ran the furniture side of the store. The woman was so very nice.

This was one of those moments that I spoke about previously where people are so kind and almost protective. We spoke at great length about my travels, and she told me about some of her own.

She had traveled all over the world. The places that stuck out in my mind was her travels overseas. She had many antiques in her store, but the way she got the items was so interesting. She had these old sewing machines that were so cool. She stated that whenever she is in another country, she would look in Dumpsters and find some really cool things. Most of the antique sewing machines she had were found in Dumpsters in other countries.

She was also a Christian woman and was not afraid to speak of her beliefs to a total stranger. We spoke about our faith. She stated that there were not very many churches around her. She had to drive about half an hour to the closest church. I finally had to get back to the car and on the road.

As I was leaving, she asked me if she could pray over me and my safe travels. There was another shopper that had come into the store that asked if she could join in the prayer. So we did just that; we prayed in the middle of the store. I was so moved that it took all I had to hold back the tears until I got into the car. God is awesome!

> You were cleansed from your sins when you obeyed the truth, so now you must show sincere love to each other as brothers and sisters. Love each other deeply with all your heart. (1 Peter 1:22 NLT)

I made my way to Lake Champlain where unfortunately I had another one of my embarrassing moments. Each trip held a multitude of memories and learning experiences. This moment was no different. Even though embarrassing, I learned a lot.

On my first trip, I purposely took a longer route around Seattle because I wanted to avoid taking a ferry. So I took a route south around Seattle.

On this trip, I wasn't so lucky. I didn't realize that I would have to take a ferry across Lake Champlain. Once I realized, I started to panic. I had no idea what to do. There were no other cars around, so I thought to myself, *I can do this, just tell the attendant that I don't know what to do.*

When I explained my stupidity, she kindly explained, "Just go up to the water, and they will tell you what to do." So that is what I did, I went up to the water. By this time, a whole line of cars started to poor in behind me right up to the water.

Finally, after about five minutes of watching two of the attendants staring and pointing at me, they approached. The lady, I might add, was quite condescending with me as she stated, "Are you going swimming?" I wasn't sure exactly what she was getting at, and I just looked at her dumbfounded. She finally said, "You are supposed to stop at the white line back there."

I just want to say, "I just did what the lady at the gate told me to," but to my further embarrassment, she made the entire line of cars, which had multiplied, back up so that I could get behind the white line. I was utterly humiliated as we waited for what felt like forever.

On the more optimistic note, I learned a valuable lesson about ferries. I will know how to take a ferry in the future.

I cut across a good portion of Vermont and New Hampshire on back highways. It was a nice change in comparison to the interstate. I drove through several quaint little towns that I now wish I had noted where I was so that I could go back and study the towns better when I got home.

As I drove through these little towns, I could feel the history, the remnants of all that had happened throughout the years, the regal churches that stood at the end of the street with its steeples rising to touch the sky.

In one town, I stopped to get gas and to use the restroom. The building was renovated into the neatest convenience store I had ever been, with its high ceilings, wide plank floors, and tall windows. It was quite different than the rundown gas stations I was used to visiting.

The only exception to this lovely drive to Maine was one of the back mountain roads that I cut across was under construction. It is not unusual to run across a lot of construction on my trips, but this road was completely torn up. I wasn't far behind the truck that was watering down the mud and sand they had just put down on the road, so needless to say, by the time I got off this road, my car was completely caked in a thick layer of gray mud. It didn't even look like my car anymore. Once I arrived in Maine, I knew that I should find a car wash as soon as possible.

I arrived in North Berwick at Georgia's house early that evening. I had never met Georgia or her family, but my mother talked of her and that side of the family often. Georgia's daughter and her husband came over, and we all went out for lobster.

You can't go to Maine and not have lobster. I wasn't really sure what to expect when we went to eat. Back in Missouri when you have lobster, it is at a nice, expensive restaurant. This wasn't the case in Maine; we went to a restaurant that was typical of a fast-food restaurant in Missouri.

The food was awesome. Of course, I had to get a whole lobster. They tried to get me to eat a lobster roll, but for my first lobster, I wanted the whole thing. I was up to my elbows in butter. Fantastic!

After we ate, Georgia's daughter took Max and me to the beach. Max loved the beach. Remember in Michigan on Lake Erie he ran from the waves. Well, that was not the case on the ocean; he ran straight for the water. We took off our shoes, and Max and I ran through the wet sand. Max kept dragging me to the water where he wanted to go swimming. I wouldn't let him swim, but he still got to play in the water. He was full of sand by the time we were finished. He found a live clam that he proudly carried in his mouth. I collected all kinds of shells, rocks, and driftwood, which is one of my favorite things to take home as souvenirs. I didn't have anything to carry it in, so I stuffed my pockets and used my shirt to carry all my treasures back to the car. My family teases me about all my driftwood in my house. I have to watch them close; they tell me they are going to stick it in my fireplace and burn it.

I really enjoyed my stay with my family. Georgia was very hospitable. Even though we really didn't know each other, they treated me just like long lost family. They opened their hearts and home to Max and me.

I loved hearing stories about my mom and my grandmother. They told me all kinds of wonderful stories that I will always treasure.

The next day, I made my way up the coast of Maine. As I stated, getting a lobster in Maine is way different. I stopped at this little place to get a lobster roll that my family told me I just had to try. It was Sunday, and I stopped at this place they told me was one of the best in Maine. The place was packed full of people. Well, that doesn't describe it very well. There was nowhere to go into; you stood in a long line and ordered at a window and waited outside along with all of the other people. There were a few tables under an awning, but there was nowhere to sit due to all of the people. Everywhere I looked, there were more and more people. That is how I usually judge the quality of an eating establishment, by the number of people. Looking at the amount of people at this place, it had to be one of the best places ever, and sure enough, it was the best lobster I have ever eaten. A lobster roll is lobster meat in a creamy mayonnaise sauce on a hoagie roll. Wow, it was mouthwatering. I sat on the back of my car with Max to eat my lobster roll, looking out at the ocean. How cool is that!

My final destination for the day was Mount Desert Island in Acadia National Park. I stayed at another KOA campsite. Of course as always, I asked for the most remote spot. The lady at the desk said there weren't really any remote spots, but one side of the campground was empty, so I would have plenty of privacy.

The lady running the campground was very nice and very helpful. I asked her if they had any butter in their little store because mine had gone bad. She explained that they had just run out. I told her that it wasn't a big deal. I would make due.

A couple hours later after setting up camp, she comes up on her golf cart with a new container of butter for me. She had gone into town and bought me some butter. I couldn't believe it.

All of the people that I come across on my trips make me want to be a better, more giving person.

I also asked the campground attendant when I checked in, if there were any hiking trails within the campground. She told me there really weren't any trails to speak of except a very short trail that ended at a small cemetery.

Now that sparked my attention; I just had to check it out. After setting up camp, Max and I walked all over the campground and then went to find that short trail. Sure enough, there was a very small, overgrown cemetery. There was only a handful of headstones that were very old.

Okay, how many of you are thinking, "Creepy!"? Exactly, I thought I would have a hard time sleeping that night, knowing about those headstones just a short walk away, but believe it or not, I was not affected.

That night, I pulled one of my embarrassing moments, and I mean really embarrassing. It was about ten o'clock, and I had just turned in after watching a movie on my laptop. I needed to use the restroom. One of the reasons I like to be in a more remote spot is that I can just get out of my car and go close by.

There is actually a couple reasons that I like to be in a remote site; I don't want to have to walk all the way back to the restrooms, and I don't really want to camp next to them. I grew up in the woods, and it doesn't bother me to squat and go.

So I get out and go behind my car to take care of business. Just as I get my pants pulled down and squat, a car pulls around the corner shining their headlights right on my hind end sticking up in the air. I was instantly mortified. I tried my best to crawl up under my car, but the damage had already been done. Talk about a full moon!

> And we know that God causes everything to work together for the good of those who love God and are called according to his purpose for them. (Romans 8:28 NLT)

It was time to start my way back home. I made it back down the coast of Maine and all the way to Sturbridge, Massachusetts. I would say that it was a good drive, but then I would be lying. The drive down the coast of Maine was nice, but as soon as I left Maine, the traffic quadrupled. To say that I don't like to drive in lots of traffic would be an understatement. This was crazy driving! I promise you this is not an exaggeration, when I went into the toll booth that had probably eight to ten booths, it was backed up with traffic. Once you left the toll booth, it was like opening the gates at a horse race. Everyone took off at top speed all in the same direction. I thought I was going to hyperventilate before I got out of the traffic. I tried to keep up, I really did, but I don't think I was doing a good job because I've never seen so many birds flying at me at once. Every car I looked at, the people were giving me their middle finger. I survived. That's all that matters. That is the worst part about going east, the amount of people in comparison to going west.

Once I made it out of the really thick traffic, I was exhausted, so I decided to pull over at a motel for the night. I had studied Sturbridge, Massachusetts, before my trip, and I thought it would be a good place to stop for the night. I am just going to tell you right now that whomever designed the streets of Sturbridge was on something that I am quite sure was not legal if you know what I mean. The streets were so confusing that I thought I was going to lose my mind. My GPS was starting to smoke because it was confused as well. I finally found a motel that had a McDonalds within walking distance. I did not want to get back into my car because I am sure that I would not find my way back to the motel. The motel was the most expensive cheap motel I had ever stayed. It was very dated but clean. The best part about it was when I opened the curtains, a small balcony overlooked a lake. It was very pretty, so Max and I ate our McDonalds outside on the balcony.

The rest of the trip home was very uneventful, and Max and I were tired and ready to be back. Once again, I was hooked. This trip was so different than the first but amazingly wonderful and educational. I learned so much about humanity and how God has made us all uniquely vital to his master plan.

FINDING MEMORIES

Wow, I can't believe it's already my third year to get to hit the open road exploring all this unique world has to offer. God is so awesome! This year, I decided that I wanted to go back to Washington, but my trip home would be different. I planned to follow the coast down Highway 101 to California to the Redwood National Forest. Now just try and tell me you are not just green with envy. Sounds like the perfect plan, right?

I don't know if I mentioned this, but when you are planning a trip of this nature, you have to be flexible. My plans got turned all caddy wonk us and all because I got too excited to get on the road. I planned the trip too early in the season, and nature got the best of me. I literally left on my trip my last day of work for my summer break and right in the middle of the rainy season. I didn't check the weather as I usually do; big mistake.

First, I hit major flooding in Iowa and was detoured all over the state. Everything was sandbagged all over the place. Finally able to get back onto I-29, I looked over, and the river to the left of me was sandbagged at least a story higher than my car. All I could think was, "If those bags give way, I am a goner. I finally made it out of the flooded areas and stopped for the night in Sioux Falls, South Dakota. I figured the first night I would get a motel because I wanted to push my driving as far as possible.

The next morning, I got up early; it was going to be a big day. I wanted to drive through the badlands and see Mount Rushmore before finding a campsite. I was so excited because I didn't do either on my first trip northwest. I made good time getting across South Dakota. Believe it or not, it felt like I had just been through that area, though it had been a couple of years.

I drove the scenic drive through the badlands, and it was so cool. It wasn't too far out of the way because I just took the back roads into Rapid City, South Dakota. I was almost too Rapid City on my way to Mount Rushmore when the ominous clouds darkened the horizon. I wasn't sure if I could make it to Mount Rushmore before the storm hit.

It was decision time: go to Mount Rushmore, hoping to make it before the storm hit or miss seeing Mount Rushmore again.

I stopped at a gas station in Rapid City while I made my decision. This is when another one of my embarrassing moments happened. To this day, I still get red in the face and that knot in the pit of my stomach when I think about what happened.

This one is going to be tough to admit, but here it goes. In setting up the scene, the gas station was very busy and crowded with cars and people alike. It was one long row of pumps, and I was in the middle.

Typically when I pump my gas, I start it and then proceed to wash my windows. I had washed the driver's side and was walking around to the other side of my car to wash the other.

There was a man yelling at someone, but I just ignored him because it was none of my business. That is until several people were yelling, and then I realized they were yelling at me. Apparently, the pump didn't stop as it normally does when it is full and was spilling all over the ground. Finally, someone had stopped it for me. Everyone at the gas station was upset with me as I am attempting to clean up the spill. There was even a sign telling you to clean up your own gas spills. I was so embarrassed.

Now I don't ever leave the pump while I am pumping my gas. I know I shouldn't have left it to begin with, but I had never had that happen. Meanwhile, the sky was now very dark, and the rain had started. I guess there was the answer to my plans for the day.

Since it was still fairly early in the afternoon, I decided to try and drive further west and hopefully out of the storm before I found a campsite. I made it as far as Gillette,

Wyoming. The storm didn't let up, and the weather prediction on the radio was tornado watches for the remainder of the evening. I guess it was another motel for me.

I decided that I should probably check the weather prediction for the next day because I would be heading into Montana. Sure enough there were torrential rains and areal flooding in the mountains of Montana. I remember the mountains on dry roads; I did not want to drive through there with areal flooding. So more big decision needed to be made. Remember, I said that you should be flexible; well, this was definitely the time to be flexible.

I decided not to go to Washington as planned. Instead, I would detour south through Wyoming to I-80 through Utah and over to Oregon to the coast where the rest of the trip would be the same as planned.

Silly Moment

As I stated, I am afraid of tornadoes and other violent storms. Well, my sister has a basement, and the boys and I were at her house when a tornado warning came across the TV. We headed down to the walkout basement of her house as we had done many other times. The boys and her husband were outside watching the sky. I decided that I was brave and went out the sliding glass door with them. I shut the screen door back but left the sliding glass door open so that we could get back in the basement. I was all brave until lightning struck a short distance away. After screaming, I found myself back in the basement. Everyone is looking at me, and my sister stated in a very dry tone, "Lena, why do you have my screen door?" Apparently, as I ran into the basement, I took the door off the track and brought it with me. So much for bravery. I have still yet to live this one down.

The next morning, God showed me again just how truly awesome he is. As you know, I stopped for the night because of the tornado watch. I am very scared of tornadoes, but this year was different since it was literally weeks since the F5 tornado ripped through Joplin divesting everything in its wake. My nerves were a little on edge to say the least.

Joplin is approximately twenty minutes from my hometown. I did not lose anyone in my close circle of family and friends; however, I knew lots of people that had lost someone or their homes on that dark day. The gut-wrenching stories encompassed my entire world for weeks. It felt good to get away from the despair, but it followed me in my heart as I drove.

Outside my motel the next morning, this very nice couple was packing up their car next to mine. We spoke briefly about where each of us was from. When I stated that I was from the Joplin, Missouri, area, the woman with a pained look on her face grabbed me in a tight hug. For the first time since the tornado, I broke down in tears. I couldn't believe myself. I think for the first time that awful event finally struck home in my heart. I knew that I was deeply saddened by all that had occurred, but the shock of it all still hadn't sunk in until that very moment. This special couple talked with me about the event and then prayed with me before parting ways. You just never know when God is going to bring one of his angels to help our hearts heal.

The day turned out to be absolutely beautiful. The weather had cleared up, and the drive was pleasant. I made my way down the middle of Wyoming and over to Utah. Driving in Utah was breathtaking and a little scary. The highway was narrow, curvy, and very busy with the red rock walls towering over you. I just held my breath and the wheel and prayed for the best.

I stopped for the night at KOA by the Great Salt Lake just north of Salt Lake City in Brigham City. The campground wasn't anything to get excited over.

I met a nice older couple that was traveling the country in their RV. Their plan was to hit every national park in the country. They had already been to most of the national parks in Utah. They gave me some pointers on where to go and where to stay.

You are probably thinking that I talk to a lot of strangers. You are right; it doesn't bother me to talk to people. That is part of the fun of taking these trips.

The next day, I made it into Oregon, where I stopped in a lovely campsite. I instantly fell in love with Oregon, and I hadn't even made it to the coast. I loved the drive, the people, the camping; everything about Oregon was fantastic. Did you know that they still have full service gas stations? I don't know if they have self-service or not, but I couldn't find any. and boy. did I try. I didn't realize that it was a full-service gas station, the first one I came to in Oregon until this man approached my car as I started to get out to pump. I thought he was coming to rob me at first, but I quickly caught on before embarrassing myself yet once again.

I can't even describe accurately how beautiful it is driving down the coast of Oregon. If you get a chance to go, I highly recommend it; it is definitely an experience of a lifetime. I stopped to camp at Cape Blanco State Park. This is by far one of my very favorite places to camp thus far. The campsite was clean and well maintained. The campsites are a little close together for my taste but still semiprivate. I could see the ocean through the trees.

Once I got my campsite set up, I decided to explore. I was backed up to some woods, so I took Max down the hill through the trees. There was a trail just down the hill a short distance. At the trail, I turned left and walked maybe two-tenths of a mile where it opened up onto a bluff overlooking the ocean. I could see a beach down to the left and a lighthouse on another bluff to the right. I went back onto the trail and took it all the way over to the lighthouse. I was able to get in a good hike and take some pictures before heading back to camp to cook dinner.

I met a couple of women and their dogs in the campsite next to mine. Turns out they were sisters from Portland, Oregon, that had just come back from the Red Wood National Forest. We visited for a long time before I retired to my car for the night. The next day, Max and I went down to the beach to play before heading out.

I was having the best couple of days. The problems with the weather were a distant memory, and things had really started looking up or so I thought. The day started out magnificently; Max and I spent the morning on the beach. I then stopped at this quaint little restaurant to eat fresh fish for an early lunch. Then I entered California, and it all went downhill from there. The atmosphere had completely changed. It started with a hateful, bitter woman at the border station checkpoint. I shrugged that off and was determined to have a great day. I almost immediately came upon redwood trees and the first campsite. I didn't want to stop just yet; I wanted to get deeper into the redwoods before setting up camp.

I had decided to stop by the time I came up to the next campsite. Along the road to the campsite, there were several cars stopped to take pictures of the elk grazing in the meadow along the road. It was pretty cool. I bet there were at least twenty elk. Once I got to the campground, I had to turn around because it was packed full and had no vacancies. No big deal. I would just go to the next.

I drove what felt like quite a ways before I saw signs for a campground in a state park. A short way down the road, a sign pointed to a dirt road that went up this mountain. I started up it and then turned around unsure of where I was going. Another car went up the road, so I decided to give it a shot. The road went six miles up this mountain and then back down. When I say road, I am using the term very loosely. The road was one lane, with major potholes and dropped off with nowhere to go but down on either side. There was a car following me that seemed to be very testy with my slow going up and down this road. Finally, I made it down the other side and came across the guard gate at the entrance. Apparently, the car behind me already had his pass to get in because he went around me and by-passed the attendant.

It all felt like slow motion as the man in the car turned and looked directly at me. Though attractive, the man sent a very uneasy vibe straight through to my core.

Through the years, I have learned to listen to those warnings that God sends to protect me. This was definitely one of those warnings. Still I shook it off and proceeded another two miles down a gravel road to the campsite.

On the way, I spotted an elk right next to the road. I stopped and got my camera out and took his picture. I promise you, he stood as tall as my car, and I drove an SUV.

The campsite was a complete disappointment because I really wanted to camp in the redwoods, and this site was right on the beach. It was cold and windy, and the sites were all open and on top of each other.

I really didn't fit in; everyone had just come back in from riding the waves. For some people, that would be so cool, but

I am just not a surfer. As I drove around the campsite, the uneasy feeling never left me. I decided to forget staying there and made my way back up the mountain and down again.

My nerves were shot, and it was getting late, so I determined that it would be a motel for the night. Now you might think that it is the end of my bad first impression of California, but it's not. When I look for a motel, I try to find something fairly inexpensive, clean, and pet friendly. I found a place in Eureka, California. I went in to check things out. The first thing I asked the man at the front desk was if they were pet friendly. He simply stated that they were. I then asked about their rates. He eyed me up and down for a moment before checking his computer. After a few minutes of searching, he turned to me with a disgusted look on his face and stated, "We don't have anything for…*you*!" I stood there with a shocked and hurt look on my face I am sure before thanking him and leaving. As I walked away, I heard the woman he had been talking to say, "Tony, I can't believe you just did that."

I thankfully made it to the car before the tears came. I called my mom bawling my eyes out about how much I hated California. I found a Motel 6 down the road a ways and hid out in my room for the night. I didn't even eat dinner that night. So much for the lovely start of my day.

The next day was much better. I drove to a scenic byway called the Avenue of Giants. It was like driving through another world. The trees really are beautiful giants. After having such a bad day the day before, my plan was to head out of California as soon as possible. The drive through the Avenue of Giants changed my mind. I really wanted to camp among the spectacular trees. I found an awesome campground, Hidden Springs Campground. I was very early getting to the campsite, and the attendant told me that check-in time wasn't until 2:00 in the afternoon. She must have felt sorry for me and told me to go ahead and pick out my site, and I could go ahead and set up for the day. I had the entire campground to myself; it was so quiet and peaceful. Max and I walked and explored every inch of the campground, and it was a large campground with 155 sites.

The next day, I headed across California along Highway 36. This road was not what I expected. It was a two-lane highway straight across the mountains with no towns for the 141 miles between Fortuna and Red Bluff.

Get ready because I am going to embarrass myself yet once again. Now when I said there were no towns, I really mean to say, there were no bathrooms for that entire time. I don't know how many of you know anything about irritable bowl syndrome, but when you have to go, you *have to go*.

It was not long after I got onto Highway 36 that I felt that rumbling feeling you get in your stomach. Within minutes, it turned into that "Oh no here it comes!" feeling. I started preparing to stop at the next town, except there was no next town. I was squirming and hurting and praying for relief. I finally thought to myself, *I can't go on!* I was going to have to go amongst the trees.

Now this was not ideal and definitely something that I did not want to do, but it had come to that point. Remember I said this was a two-lane highway, well what I didn't tell you is that there were no shoulders either, and the road was very, very, very curvy. So pulling off to the side just wasn't in the cards. However, every now and then, there were a few places that had a little pull off, so I stopped at the next one that I came to with the intention of squatting behind the nearest tree out of sight. I waddled my way over to the tree line, moaning the entire way just to find that the ground went straight down. I am good, but I was pretty sure that I could not hold onto a tree and go at that angle. In fact, I was pretty sure that I couldn't even stand at that angle. So I waddled my way back to the car, once again praying for relief the whole way. Finally after several more miles, I came across a laundry mat and three porta-potties, and they were my best friend. God does answer prayers!

Things were much better after Red Bluff. Now don't get me wrong; everything in Northern California was beautiful. Highway 36 was crazy before Red Bluff with the curves. The one time I stopped on the pull off, a car came whizzing around the corner up on two wheels. It scared me half to death. I am not sure how fast they were going, but I am surprised they didn't wreck their little black car. The car was full of teenagers out for a joy ride. I know they survived because I passed them coming back the other way.

Growth of a Tree

It was an exhausting day, and even though I had a bit of trouble that morning, Northern California was definitely worth experiencing. Yes, I do want to go back again.

The last leg of my trip, I took I-40 back east. I stopped by to see the Grand Canyon as I went through.

The gentleman earlier in my trip in Utah told me that it will look exactly like every picture I have seen of the Grand Canyon; the difference is the overwhelming feeling you will experience. He was right; it almost brought tears to my eyes because it is an obvious display of God's awesome power.

This was my biggest trip yet, and I loved every bit of it. I had so many wonderful experiences that the memories will last me a life time.

> O Lord, our Lord, the majesty of your name fills the earth! Your glory is higher than the heavens. (Psalms 8:1 NLT)

FINDING GOD'S STRENGTH

My journey is not the same as your journey; the point is to take the journey. Live your life to the fullest. Live your life as if there is no tomorrow. It doesn't matter what your journey holds as long as you are taking it and not waiting for life to happen for you.

Remember that just because you are putting yourself out there and trying to live your life to the fullest doesn't mean that it is always going to be fun and games. God never promised that life will be full of roses. You will still have hard times. Those are the most important times in your life. Those are the times that you are going to grow and learn. Just understand that it is how you handle those tough times that define you as a person. You can either give into it or let it beat you or you can stand up and take control of the person you want to become.

You have now seen that I have tried to put my children's needs before my own, I have gone back to school and found a career, and I have learned how to have fun. I wanted to share my experience with my travels because first of all, I learned how to have fun, but I have also grown as a person and grown closer to God through the people that he put in my path along the way. There is a huge world out there full of God's children ready to open their arms and welcome you.

Look within yourself; find who you are as a person, the person that is waiting to get out and live life to the fullest. You don't have to settle for just anyone to start living your life. You don't have to resort to drugs and alcohol to escape a lonely life. You don't have to stay with someone who abuses you on a daily basis. You don't have to feel miserable in life just because you are single.

As I have stated, I do not condone divorce. I am not encouraging you to live a life of solitude. God wants us to find a partner, to find love. I hope that you find the love of your life, to find your soul mate.

I know there are a lot of you out there, male and female alike that are alone and lonely. Trust me when I say that even though you are alone, you don't have to be lonely. God will take the lonely away and give you peace with who you are as a person.

Don't wait for someone else to start living your life. You deserve to find the wonderful, marvelous person that you are down inside. Get to know who you are, and spread your wings for all to see.

It is taking me a long time to find love, but I will never give up hope. Notice that I said "is" taking me a long time. No, I still haven't found the love of my life. I know that love awaits me. I don't know when or how I will find the man that will someday be my partner in life, but I have faith that it will happen. Until then, I am going to be content with who I am and the life that I live.

My story is far from over, as is with your story. That is the beauty of life; it is ever changing and growing. There is still a lot more in life for me and for you to experience.

God has put us on this earth for a microsecond in eternity, and we have to make the most of what he has given us until the very end, when we get called home to be with him.

The point in all of my rambling is that no matter what curve ball life has thrown, causing you to be alone, don't fret. God will always be there to give you the strength and courage to do anything that you want to do as long as it is in his plan. Trust in him, for you can do all things through him!

> For I can do everything with the help of Christ who gives me the strength I need. (Philippians 4:13 NLT)

Shout with joy to the Lord, O earth! Worship the Lord with gladness. Come before him, singing with joy. Acknowledge that the Lord is God! He made us, and we are his. We are his people, the sheep of his pasture. Enter his gates with thanksgiving; go into his courts with praise. Give thanks to him and bless his name. For the Lord is good. His unfailing love continues forever, and his faithfulness continues to each generation. (Psalms 100 NLT)